Look Closer

Contents

Alison Blank

OXFORD

Introduction

The world is full of many living things. Some are large, some are small. Some are so tiny you can't see them with your eyes alone.

Look closer and you will discover just how amazing these tiny things can be!

On the body

These are human eyelashes. They keep things from getting in your eyes.

Look closer …

Through a **microscope** you can see tiny **mites**. They live on human eyelashes! We all have them. You can't see or feel them and they don't do you any harm.

In the mouth

How clean do you think these teeth are?

Through a microscope you can see the **microbes** that live in your mouth. These microbes love sugar. When you eat sugar the microbes make a sticky **film** that grows on your teeth. The film can make holes in your teeth. It can also harm your **gums**.

Brushing your teeth helps to get rid of these microbes.

Microbes on a tooth

On the hands

Do these hands look clean to you?

Through a microscope you can see the microbes that live on your skin. Most don't bother you. Some even help you. But some microbes can make you sick. We call these **germs**.

Washing your hands is the best way to stop germs spreading.

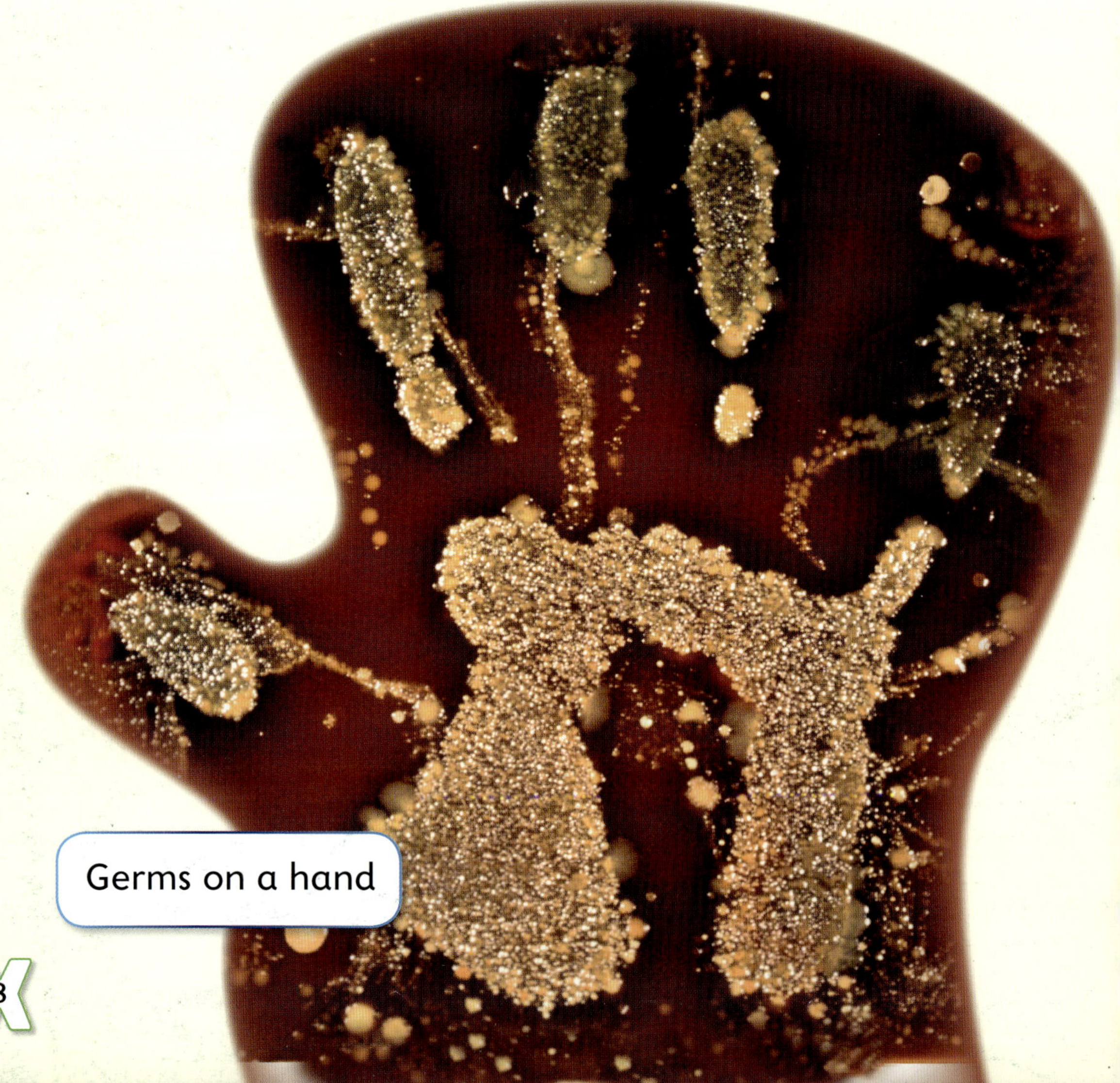

Germs on a hand

In the bedroom

This bed looks soft and ready to sleep on.

dust mite

Through a microscope you can see tiny dust mites. They live on pillows and in mattresses. Dust mites eat bits of old skin.

A mattress can have as many as 10 million mites living in it!

In the kitchen

This is a bowl of **dough**. Dough is baked to make bread.

Look closer ...

Through a microscope you can see yeast at work. Yeast is made up of microbes. The microbes eat the sugar in the dough. They make gas which causes the dough to expand. Yeast makes the bread light and fluffy.

Yeast microbes

These microbes can also change milk into yoghurt and cheese.

In the garden

Many animals live in our gardens.
This squirrel looks cute and fluffy.

Through a microscope you can see his fleas! Fleas live in the fur of many animals, like squirrels. The fleas bite the animals and make them itch. Fleas can carry disease.

In the park

This tree stump looks dead but it is alive with living things.

Glossary

dough	a mixture of flour and liquid used for baking
film	a very thin layer
germ	a tiny creature that causes disease
gum	soft part of your mouth that attaches your teeth to your jaw
microbe	a tiny creature
microscope	an instrument that makes tiny things look bigger
mite	a tiny creature

Index